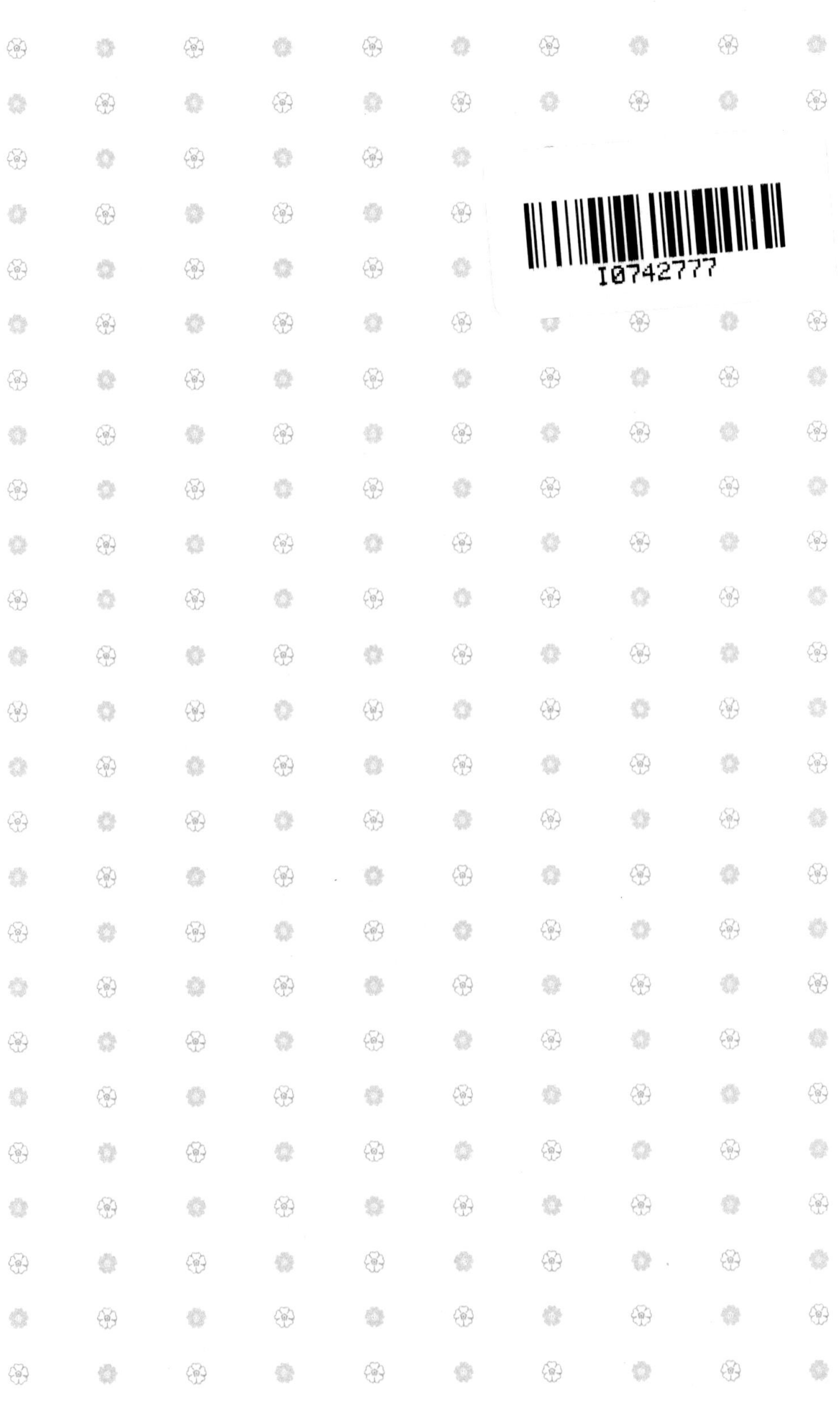

I0742777

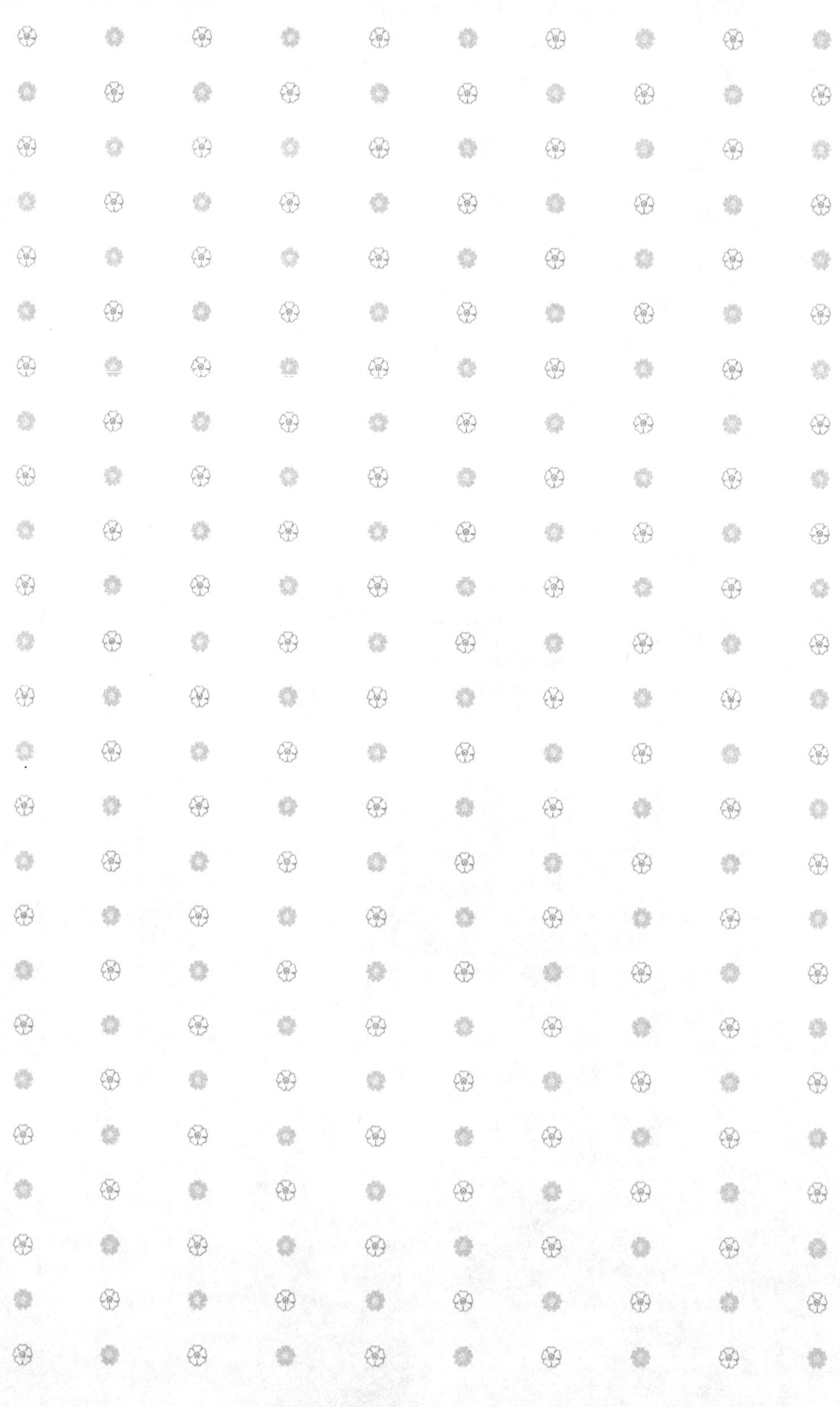

in case of emergency press

We are proud to acknowledge the Traditional Owners of
country throughout Australia and to recognise their
continuing connection to land, waters, and culture.
We pay our respects to their Elders.

We support recognition, reconciliation, and reparation.

A Material Rain

Jonas Kyle-Sidell

in case of emergency press
https://icoe.com.au
Travancore, Victoria
Australia

Published by in case of emergency press 2023

ISBN: 978-0-6458496-8-4

Cover design: Ward Nikriph

Acknowledgements

My whole messy family. You know who you are. The Maryland Zoo in Baltimore, and my friends from the Horticulture Department, where I worked when this book was written.

Bernie Sanders and the Political Revolution. You inspired millions; it took an entire ruling class to hold you back. This book is about appealing to peoples' real lives—in politics, in education, in art. Only then can we listen. Only then can we lead. Only then can we inspire. Only then can material conditions change. It will not come from experts, it'll only come from us.

For all the independent news outlets which buck the oligarchy and keep us alive, especially during dark days like the pandemic, when conspiracy is so easily drawn upon. And especially during normal times, when conspiracy is so easily dismissed.

We are allowed to ask for more. It is allowed to be simple.

It must mean something.

Dedication

Addie, Mason, and Miles, for meeting me where I am

Table of Contents

A Material Rain

Jonas Kyle-Sidell

Prologue

The light is shinning into the backyard. The neighbors are having a party. Grandfather and children and their children. The little girl wails, "WEEEEEEEEEEEEEEE!" as she runs after a ball in their backyard with no fence, just a slope rolling into that of the other house behind it. Some great music is playing—Tupac, along with some real R&B.

The grandmother died a couple years back. We knew neither of them very well, except for the coming and going greetings, to and from each other's cars, or the over-the-fence banter. She the talker—colloquial, some sass, you could tell. Him, slower moving, more of a nod-and-peer-over-the-glasses type. One day we came home and he came up to us and said she had passed. "Liver cancer. It was very aggressive." It was the most he had said to me in a while.

Shortly after, I remembered a night I had stepped outside. It was very dark and I must've been smoking a joint and drinking a beer, and as I was heading back in I noticed what looked like a woman's figure standing on the porch. She startled me, seemed to pop out of the dark, some hair and elbow and what looked like a broken stance, head in a hand or arms gripping each other. I swear I saw the hair blow a little in the night air. In my memory after the grandfather told me, as in the moment, I wasn't even sure I saw her. But I do remember a woman bent off the end of that porch, like someone bent to sea. Maybe it was her daughter, stepping out to fall apart before going in to regain her composure. Maybe it was the grandmother herself, trying to hold and shed this harrowing sorrow: that this night, behind her house—maple trees, soft sounds of a few teenagers on the basketball court across the street, just a wisp under the sky but the corners of her precious freedom in life—that this that was hers, would go on without her.

And she was gone. And this fourth of July a couple years later the grandfather had been working all week and playing his lovely music, pressure washing the deck for the kids and grandkids. They all flow to the front yard, as do we, when a slew of unofficial fireworks light up the night sky over the basketball court and all over the county.

The canna lilies, out front, and raised bed summer squash out here don't ask for permission, they just grow. The coronavirus didn't ask us if it could come and steal all our oxygen, it just came—likely because we were stealing that of Planet Earth's. The sky didn't ask Yvonne if she was done looking at it, or the sunlight, or the cool grass—

As a teacher, I want to make my students less afraid of their own words, and to feel part of a tradition of expression. The form will beat you down enough, and if anything, we can change it! Society reflects us, not the other way around. The extent to which we must mirror it is the extent to which we must survive, but that is no way to be great. Or even happy?

"Can I cuss in my essay?" "Yes."

And that is what was so potent about Bernie Sanders' campaign—a politician with the soul of a teacher—and the movement that launched it and the movement that continues. We did not have to indoctrinate ourselves in the institutions; we could embody them. We are healthcare. We are education. We are criminal justice reform. We are climate change. We are poetry. We are literature. And this is what *we* deserve about it.

And then, like the carved out shell of a summer squash, the charade of neoliberal electoral politics held. Ironically— almost as punishment for refusing to de-commodify our human rights and the planet—this happened just as we are thrown into the well of COVID-19, where the ground swell of progressive ideas is like a dusty ray of moonlight, now, rolling right over the junipers and into my backyard. For a moment, I think I see a woman on my neighbors' porch again.

I'm becoming so tired of being afraid. Afraid of losing my parents. Afraid of my son losing me. Afraid of losing myself. The fireworks tonight, and of American exceptionalism, are over, and it's time to go in. But—now more than ever—let us remember and hold a place of power, where we are not relegated to the lesser of two evils, where we do not litigate lies, but speak the truth about a fallen empire, failed state that got us here, and work for an economy that explodes from the guts of our lyrical humanity, not the recesses of continued compromise and commodified interests. Let us love and let us play and when it's all over, like a river, let it simply cease to be.

"Let us try to assume our fundamental ambiguity. It is in the knowledge of the genuine conditions of our life that we must draw our strength to live and our reason for acting."

Simone de Beauvoir

The Stranger

Like boneset
set to a still tune

of sunlight,
desperadoes in the morning dew,

fuzzy white tips
lonesome against a clear blue sky

on this
dyin' planet...

There's never been anything wrong with bein' wrong about it—

those who can embrace the stranger
can embrace the facts:

if we're not here by design,

we're just here.

My own Democracy

The Light

It is hard

to live within

time—it is

even harder

knowing eventually

we will become it.

The Dead and the Powerful

If greed
is the low living embodiment

of the continued compromise of our highest ideals—

for ourselves, for our country—

of our powerlessness—
against the media,

against racism, against sexism,

against war, against truth,

against the few who thrive

on a broken system
for the many—then order

similarly
disembodies me. The Democratic Party

would rather lose an election

than lose the party, but as voters
we're supposed to be more responsible.

Fuck that—

this is how we got here.

When does it end?

My vote
is not an abstraction

any more than Jim Clyburn taking more money

than any other person in Congress from the Pharmaceutical
industries

is. I
have had it—

but I'll take the revolution of smog clearing

from people staying home. I'll take the crushing index of
progress

that comes with historical pain. Nobody knows
what's other side the paint—

in the annals of the future, we await.

For Love

The young people
are right,

maybe this
will wake us up, maybe this

will make us
think about

global warming,
the power

of nature,
people

over profits.
Maybe this

can bring us
together. Last I heard

this may last
two years. Thank you

for your
bright disruption

that will lead us
in this

new dark reality.
The kids are alright,

the magnolias are blooming,
we are all

in this
together.

My Own Democracy

It has hit
home. No not some

faraway land. People are dying
outside my window.

Yet I sing, to you
in here. No not from some

radical point of view, just me
and my

yellow legal pad, and the knowledge
that *we are not safe.* Easy for one to see now

the beneficiaries
of our

But there's a bird outside my window,

popular disenchantment, and the byzantine system
which creates it, like a child

afraid to ask for more. We have been shamed
into a freedom that thinks

deductibles are a natural part
of health insurance—   that thinks

some men deserve our silence
while others

our moral superiority—   that thinks
paid sick leave

is too much to ask—   that thinks
education

is a crime, and a prison system—the largest
in the history

of the world—   that thinks
the planet, like democracy, is not ours

to save. Too faraway. Well here we are. We have quashed
the latest

social
movement, in favor of

                    telling me to love

adulting. Our individualized
economy

is flailing, struggling
to account

for everybody. I open my window
and let

the socialist winds
blow over

                even when we disagree, to fly,

the blinking lights
of our capitalist landscape,

its hills and valleys, its beauty—
but *suddenly cold to pandering,*

            even when we bleed, and she's tellin' me

wizened to the truth—
its hollow veins,

deep cracks in the open roads
and commitments   of trees

                it's mine.

Parable of the Lesser of Two Evils

Spent my life
thinkin' a winnin',

trying to be free, but
'long the way

everything told me
to be anything

but me. In school
they said

my grammar was incorrect.
Doctors

tol' me I was fat. So
I got a job

standin'—employer said
I was lucky for that—and I

stayed
for 50 years. 'Til one day

I *punch my boss*
in the face,

come home,
eat a bag of chips,

sit down, and write
this poem.

The Ruling Class

They weren't afraid
love couldn't win,

they were afraid
love would win. For them—

greed is the lesser evil, and order
is just around

to perpetuate this lie.
What we want, as

workers, as patients, as students—
is not money, health, or knowledge—

as activists, as poets, as citizens—
is not prestige, eternity, or safety—

is power. To not be sold
the same fucking crime.

None but, the issues
of our time.

My family
is my political inspiration.

Medicare for all, Green new deal,
Wealth tax, free college, student loan

forgiveness, legalized weed, prison and immigration
reform, the river of pain keeps

rolling on

The Defector

It was a quiet moment
at dusk

at the very beginning of summer
when I defected.

Just my son
who keeps getting older

in the stroller,
just my roller.

The houses
like tinker boxes

lamp shades behind shades
in the night.

And I remember
when I learned

the power of the written word,
how it sliced

through the dark,
through my mind,

the shooting star
it left behind.

The Fiddle

Emperor Nero—as Rome burned—the year 64 AD,
played the fiddle. Perhaps

it applied some sense of order. Our response
has been the same. We all watched it

happen. The candidates / cops lap up
the platform of love, then twist it like a curve ball,

aiming
to paint it immoderate. Over and over. But, as the fiddle

continues to play, we have descended
that bullshit cross, again, into the streets, hopefully

for real this time. Let's
let it spill out, the high notes of pragmatism be damned.

You Can Have It

Oligarchy Pandemic Blues

That one
unsparing
voice, redolent,
necessary. Prophetic
fightback
noise—
joy
in the unsparing—

this unseasonable
desperate
feeling,

like the fires
stretching

from San Diego to Canada,
Kenosha to Minnesota,
Florida to Iowa to New York
to Washington, DC, etc.
The neoliberal order
cannot respond.
So fascism
is.
So militarism
will.
So nonviolent democratic revolution
must.

One can only hope
these articles are still around

to rejoice in the aftermath,
and progress that invariably follows,

but right now, the seasons are
changing again,

                    and the zelkovas,
the beeches, the poplars, honey locusts,
mulberries, redbuds, and oh
the redwoods, pines, and sequoias!

They are not asking
for our law and order. No. Not even close.

Our Justice

Can't breathe
when 53 cents in the dollar

goes to militarism
at home and abroad,

speaks the word *poverty*,
is a movement

rooted in policy
that roots out corruption

lest we roll over
when faced with temptation,

a moment, however fleeting,
rooted in history

like a bird
caught by the song on the wind

that sings of humanity,
does not negotiate

with those
whose ideas and identities

would form
off truncating

ours, whose very existence
breathes

vis-à-vis
our suffering.

Cry Hypocrite

I was despondent.
Milquetoast, moribund.
Spending my time
crying hypocrite, taking no risks,
while blowing the status quo.

       (A horn song.)

It was a privileged position, to pretend
to be able to play both sides
without offending anybody. Unsurprisingly,
I didn't have much to say, and spent my time
crying hypocrite, placing no bets,
and blowing the status quo.

       (A horn song.)

It was a couple of books, or a mass movement,
that knocked me down to size. I was jubilant, flawed!
would rather die trying, break
from feeling, than spend my time
crying hypocrite—*anything*
but lonely, blowing up the status quo.

       (A horn song.)

Something that pre-empts, and rebukes
tyranny—
not mediocrity—
a greatness, like art, bringing justice
to the condition
of being human.

Suburbia

Is there a reason
for the fashion

of the season,
a product or agitator,

a boat adrift?
Everybody hates

the radical left.
What pins you

to such separateness,
such exclusivity,

such anti-society,
that which makes you

uniquely American?
Your (tax) plan

is unsustainable
without grifting

from those
you are keeping out.

Was it the
HOA or

House Committee
on Un-American Activities

that made you
afraid of

any kind of
universal

equity? Does your coffee
taste like xenophobia? Do

the shutters
keep out

class politics? Everybody hates
the radical left.

Apropos of a Lie

An empire
abhors transparency—
so the little bombs
Julian Assange
and Edward Snowden
dropped. So the direct threat
of good music.
Of socialism, honest programs—
the apropos
of a lie—only confusion
is necessary
for the dirty little secrets
to pass. So the convenience
of a historically disenfranchised
people, shadowy
neglect. But the Democrats
can't hide anymore
behind the institutions
they cited. It is burning
before our eyes. And their ideology
has consolidated
like that of Republicans did
in the seventies
behind a spiteful
gaze. And those of us
who would resurrect the institutions—
the seventy percent
of the country:
women, people of color
under thirty-five
who agree

on most subjects of power
are called
radical, like children
scolded behind the veneer of tranquility.
The only thing
more dangerous
than that
is struggle.

Schoolyard Democracy

Don't pretend
the sun

        If empathy

is not full of pain—
do not

        is prophecy, and democracy

tell me
your political incontinence

        needs a schoolyard,

and impotence
have anything

        and demagoguery

to do
with anything—what's your economic

        forms

plan? What a fucking
shame. You won

        out of a need

because of us, not in spite of us, but your
pathetic

        to believe in something

outlook
can't figure it. Subject

      when the crops are dyin',

popular
policies

      then don't piss on me

to ruthless platitudes,
and you, my friend,

      and call it rain.

will rue the day

God is a Demagogue

And I am a socialist.
And love is an atheist,
and truth
is pleasure
and pain, a material rain—not that
which never
arrives.

Our Promise

The sun
was a golden husk.
The sky
blue
like evergreen.
My love
was not in a rut.
My friends
were gathered around.
I won
all the preliminary rounds.
But after a faked injury, and pack
of lies, he bought
his way
into the finals. Unfortunately,
he also bought the crowd's sympathy.
But I stole their hearts. By the end,
when I sank that last shot,
like our promise—not our shadow,
and he cried
foul
again,
nobody
fucking
cared.

The Rest is History

I was a kid
in California. A bicycle
outside the Beverly Center. A long reed
inside a tenor sax
leading to 3rd St.
The day
would not go away,
holding back the night,
inoculating
like a screened-in porch
and light beer
in Georgia.
Like a sun burn
radiating
against streetlight.
A pandemic
like a piano
on our heads, the flat sound
of a punch line, a once
revolution, everything
that coulda been, that spits us out, now,
into infamy
along that ancient highway.
A freezing rain
of the last winter
like misinformation
and middle age, a political culture
buttressed by tokenism,
void of policy
even during a plaque.
More than World War 2,

a 9/11 every day, yet we can't
turn our eyes towards suffering,
a country that's reeling,
a system that's failing.
The sounds of shame
cast in stone
and guilt, like a temporary fix,
the rolling sky
remembering hunger, shackles, barbarism.
We need a moral scalpel
to remove the rot of ages,
national psychotherapy,
to fall in love with democracy again,
not pageantry. You can't plan it away
or protect it
without risking losing it. It should survive
a stampede, a slogan, a cynicism, a profiteering.
It requires a leap of faith, inspiration, does not live
in the mediocre realm of fact, decision, or precision.
For it is big, bold, broad, and messy—but simple
and profound, like hiding a joint
behind your ear. My son, like an entry point
into the inchoate scenery. Like remembering the world
before we came to it, this way, when I was yet
a ray of light
bleating upon it.

A Blues for My Son

I want
you
to come at
the world,
not it
at you—
to know
the politics
of failure,
because failure
is politics,
if I had been
successful
right away,
I can't imagine
I ever
would have
been awake
enough, or
perhaps
angry
enough
or
disenchanted
enough
to care, to
need it, to
need
something.
Now
take that to mean

what you want.
I wouldn't have
eschewed
success, not
with women, not
with writing, but
I'm telling you
it has made me
stronger. One
realizes
one thing: optimism
can only
be blind. And that
truly is
radical, and it is
so
scary
for those
who have built
themselves
up
around the idea
of measured
risk—and more
so—
made a mockery
of those
who would travel
full of fervor, amidst
this carelessness. You can't
hate the rain,
because it's falling.
You can't
love
the sun

too much
or it
will fry you.
You can't
hate the population,
because it's multitudinous.
You can't
support a broken, racist,
classist
wheel,
but
you can
walk, even in the snow.
Truth
is the sound
of platitudes
breaking,
like glass. You can't
dismantle
the power
structure, any more
than you can take on
death,
but, as it turns
out, you can laugh.

The Populist

You needn't be versed
in poetry, any more
than a tree, be leaved
in leaves. Any more
than the sky, learning
to fly. Any more
than the sidewalks
can un-ramble
and meander less,
or the road
itself
could stop
going. The birds
do not have master's
degrees.
The ordinary salve
of passion, the right to care
beyond attribution. We defy
academic orthodoxy
because spare me. The prosaic
nature
of the problem
repudiates that.
It is a learned
helplessness, trained
subservience, telling us
that to be unswerving
is to be insolent—that
if only we work hard
enough, we could be
as egalitarian

as you. Not that
we already
are. And then someone
comes along—out of this dissolved
population, and consciousness—and says,
the trees
butter
for you too. The rain
smells of salt, and the highlights
in your hair
could decrease profit margins
by a horizon and a half, and most
certainly, they cannot
have it all, and if
so, well, *you*
can have it.

43

The Long Day

Weed Wackin'

Today, I'm just a painter—
tasked

to see, as if
this could bring forth being.

Find, stop, invoke time,
like my California childhood,

or the way sunlight,
through a temperate day,

'cross his amber skin, now,
does.

Today, I'm just a musician—
consoling a moment

for what eternity
won't be haggled down for.

Today, I'm just a gardener,
drinking blueberry beer,

talking to termites,
giving them my best lesson

in weed wackin'
and ethnobotany.

COVID *is still burning,*
capitalism is falling,

the cicadas are coming—the roses
out front

look best
beat up

against a splotched, rolling sky.
Mornings deserve

music. Always, I will be your father,
chasing down the love,

we cannot conquer.

The Moon as a Ball in the Sky

Doesn't
think like a streetlight, just

lights up the night, doesn't
burn like the sun, just

can't see it
as patently separate.

Is not political, just
can't be pigeon-holed—

it's quite simple!—is not
radical at all. And the moon

is a ball
in the sky, concerns

everyone, if ya ain't
got a story, charged

with the time.
I just want a good song

to shunt the tide,
never had a reason

to lie,
let the rain in.

Never had a need
to belong, *like dust on the windowpane.*

I belong
to the idea

that we all want the same things.

Is not political, just
can't be pigeon-holed—

it's quite simple! is not
radical at all. And the moon

is a ball
in the sky, concerns

everyone, if ya ain't
got a story, charged

with the time.
There's not much left

at the end of our fears,
just the sound

of children laughing,
just an ordinary song

of populism
that has been turned

on its head, as if—
broadly speaking—we cannot

speak broadly—
as if it is all not

just above our heads. Just the same
pandemic blues, now,

one hundred years later,
just the moon

as a ball
in the sky, concerns

everyone, if ya ain't
got a story, charged

with the time.

When My Time Comes

I know
we haven't

known each other
too well—

but I know
my mom

considers herself
to be

a lot like you, and likewise,
I consider myself

a lot like her. This means
I must be

a lot like you.
I hope that's true. Because

I want to believe
I will be

as brave
as you.

The birds
dived

and wrestled
in the mulberrys. "I'sorry birdies," he says,

the next day, remembering
their trajectory.

We are out there, doing the same thing. And the next
day,

I am at work, and it is a moment
I can't get out of, the wind

blowing through the beeches, my feet
planted

where they can find traction. Fear—
that nimble

beast, not able
to find

any—pushed up
against

that mirror, just dust
and stars.

As America Continues On

Those moments
when the light
gets beyond oneself.

For instance, heaving mulch
through a crowd.
or when a little one

plants themself
inside your life.
Now this is not the innocence

Baldwin speaks of—
that refuses to grow up.
This is the kind

that spots the distance,
and transmogrifies
the light,

we know that racism is bad
for all of us,
except the ruling elite.

That punchline
that pits us
against each other.

Privilege
that is as undeserved
as pain,

pushing us
away from universality,
towards marginality.

We are all cloaked in it—
waiting for some light
to break.

And then—not without resistance—
it does, old Time,
dancin' outside the window.

I Hope it's not Too Late

For the trees,
for the kids,
for the liver,

for the bees,
the entrenched powers,
for the river...

they remind us
what it's like
to throw a ball
in the air—

as inequality
spins
like a figure skater
on the evening news.
For the possible politician

to give us
one more
watery gem

before a prostrate
Congress, as global catastrophe
looms. As capitalism

coagulates,
like oil in a Petri dish,
it has no memory, no fight,

unable to explain,
why it can't explain—

a system
with no self-reflection
is cold and lonely. If it's too late

for establishment politics—then it's time
for poetry,
for rock'n'roll,

for a *bluesmanship*, humiliated and *hangry*
for light. Let's make it too late
for conspiracy theories. Too solid

for division
from up top. Too soon
for racism, misogyny, censorship. Time

for progressive policy! Too late, too late, now,
for demagoguery. As the gates of summer

have opened—
and the neighborhood
is *alive*
with balls in the air!

a teeming warmth
of work and play,

bodies bopped
in the slow dusk, bright
with the cost of living.

The Long Day

With its
ever-evolving

stimulus,
brings demagogues

to their knees.
Because truth

is more powerful
than the status quo.

And if you can't find
a critique of capitalism,

then you've been
staring at the sun.

But do not shame,
never censor—

that kind of love
could take down

empires.
A child's love

is not tough—
it is patient,

it has time.
We

are on the clock,
the way a sunset

reveals, and mornings
conspire. And if you can't find

a way to be both,
then you're

running out of time.
Do not shame, never censor,

that kind of love—
could take down empires.

You got your toys,
I got your dreams,

I wish our leaders
had your mistakes,

'cause I just saw, now,
in your

face, a sadness,
they ain't never dared

feel. Do not shame, never
censor, that kind of love

could take down empires.

Let Me Sing a Simple Song of Work

That doesn't
have to, and always
has to.

So that I never
take for granted
the sweat

on someone else's
back.

Perhaps capitalism
codifies racism,
which in turn
conditions us
for capitalism.

Let me sing
a simple song
of work.

Something about the way
the air
stills—
as if
time
is palpable.

My childhood
long gone,
I have a child

of my own
now.

I hear
a woodpecker—
on a poplar—
somewhere—

let me sing
a simple song
of work.

Over half a million
gone, we can't
give everybody

a job
who wants one, I said

over half a million
gone, we can't
give everybody

a job
who wants one.

The seeds
of racism
are sown
of a system
which thrives
for the few
off inequality
for the many.

The cicadas
coming up
like voices
of the dead.

Sustainability Blues

The sky is a muster,
rollicking sea

of pain,
everybody on their porches,

sittin' rain.
The law is a huckster,

criminally
insane,

people packed in jail cells,
sittin' rain.

Wanna know
how we got here?

Let's go back to 1970
when we drained

the public pool...
Racism

drained the pool.
Scared white people

privatized this nation.
Now we all

pay more, now we all
pay more. Division

victimizes
any

population. Wanna know
who benefits

from such
incrementalism? Just the few,

just the few...
Love

is a bumper,
a used car

in the rain,
can't expect a ride,

ya ain't
willin' to change.

Wanna know
why we can't

have nice things? Let's go back
to the moment

we called ourselves
kings. The sky

is a muster,
rollicking sea

of pain,
everybody on their porches,

sittin' rain.

Tree of Heaven

The mundane
is the only truth

like a slanted walk.
Truth

is the only universal
like a tree

of heaven. The universal
is magic, like time

passing—
just like that

everything's
changed. Work hard,

maybe someday
get ahead. The politics

is that
of coming together. The rest

is a media coup
of lies

to protect
the wealthy

and forget about:
the old man

on MLK
with one leg

wheeling his chair
through traffic.

Walk with me under this
tree of heaven,

long time
passing.

If you believe in
street art, then

you believe in
grassroots politics.

If you believe
everybody's

a victim
of war—

you believe in
peace,

not racism. The rest
is a media coup

of lies
to protect

the wealthy
and forget about:

the old man
on MLK

with one leg
wheeling his chair

through traffic.
Walk with me under

this tree of heaven,
long time

passing. No cheap labor
in this tree of heaven,

honest reporting
in this

tree of heaven,
no scapegoating

in this
tree of heaven.

Long time
passing—

Fealty

Those Without a Country

The missiles don't know
if they're misguided;

separate together
leads to dominance,

this is just a mix—
a one-state solution

where the old thinking
is the problem. Brothers and sisters,

we can't
capitalism our way out

of this
anymore. There has to be room

for collective cooperation. You can't
adjust

for inequity, only give it
to everybody. When I see a cherry tree,

blooming on an old street,
it almost feels

like ecstasy, saxophone
mimicking the wind

eternally. Last night,
I sat with my son

as he fell asleep, and tried to imagine
what it would be like

if bombs were falling. What will it take
to un-support nationalism, de-victimize

the conqueror, expatriate
this zero-sum game? Those without a country

must know. Same way
a missile, a knee on the neck,

tear gas, chokeholds, checkpoints,
poverty, occupation, apartheid, don't. Those without a country

must know
those with a country

will never be free, *as long as I, a black person, a
Palestinian, am dictating policy. Maybe that's why*

they hate me. Because I am their country.
I am your country,

mimicking the wind
eternally. Blowing through the rubble,

after they just killed
my family, marching through the streets,

blowing through
your neighborhood, now

Fealty

I need a poem
to save the day—

       I need a moment

the end
of summer
is coming quickly,

       aligned with my fealty:

and I already miss the starlight,
already miss

       the sky, the birds, a song

the kid
bouncing his ball
in the evening's light,

       drifting

walks to the store,
the campfires,

       cross the wet pavement.

I can't take it, sometimes—
don't know what to do
about time,

       Some notion of possibility

'bout your eyes
and mine.

       stirring me

The Caged Bird

Today, gonna put off
the whole world.

Let it sweat
before it shines.

Take my money
to the central bank—

write my kids
a check,

buy myself
a drink.

Go home,
stare listlessly

at the summer passing,
the caged bird

singing
from the mezzanine

*the slow dance
of time,*

shaking
my speakers...

Tonight,
the planet

heaves
a hot sigh,

as another
neoliberal

president
signs

an oil contract...
demagoguing

our dreams,
like brandishing

color
from turpentine.

The blue sky
thinning,

parents
getting old,

children
growing up,

singing:
as long

as there is
hunger

there will be
love.

News of the Day

It's about controlling time,
and *not*—

blowing down Buffalo Yard Rd.,
tap tap

of the mind,
beeches hustling

in the long summer's wind—
there's no Art—

only *rot*—
only making a living

like nutsedge
reproduces

when you pull it up—
the long road

is a good one.
Livin' fast

ain't easy, and nothin's
free. That's why

there ought to be
human entitlements

that secularize society
against greed; against the dogmas

presented
by race and class—

vis à vis
poverty—

and the news of the day.
Words becoming meaningless

like summer ending,
just a turn and a glance

down that   long   dark   hallway

The Way the Rose Bush Flutters

And I've arrived
here,
like mountains
stumbling,
the sky
crumpled,
then flattened

into ramblings
worth saving.

Beat boxing
time
into submission,

a gentle rain.

Artistic dream
running like a fox
for the field—

I would say the same thing
again—things happen

when you least look at them—

only feel it—and understanding
comes after: but tomorrow

amidst all these
existential clouds

we can only
use our hands.

Recalcitrant

I want to be released
from memory,

like a bird
in the trees,

objectified, like a dot
on the concrete,

ossified, like a fossil, then thrown
into the sea! Reality

is humiliating. Let me fall
with the branches, and run

with the bees, roll
with the rocks—

I've had it with COVID—
I'll take the slime

on the back
of an amphibian, that weed

though the crack
of the neighborhood street. I'll be dawn

as the earth spins, how 'bout that? The red cheek
of a baby. I'll be wheels

and the smell of gasoline
and the apple

that you're eating, the kickup of dirt and dust
as you peel—I'll be the *manner*

in which
each of us

does everything, just not the tenor
of need. Ain't nothin' wrong

with a vaccine
mandate, but people remember

the surprise hospital bills, loan servicing
fees. The problem is an untrustworthy

government, missing
the tenor

of need, so that
one—like me—would rather

secede
than suffer

one more
humiliation,

and you shame shaming me.
When will this country

finally allow
for a little patriotism,

built on
self-criticism

and loving people, bobbing, like a buoy
in the mist, the free market

fundamentalists
captured, the hypocrites

they are.

The Lobbyist

I exist
in the hollowed-out form
of human decency—where government
should be.

So close am I
to a poet
that I can creep inside
a husk
and fill it up,

using the language
of the oppressed,
like a perfect consumer.

You see, I'm a free market
fundamentalist; I've gotten pretty good
at being dispassionate.

Big government disguised
as little government, or vice
versa, it don't matter—
I don't exist,
like angels,
or a unicorn,

but my fiat currency
is brandished
as your gold standard
(yeah, I'm that sneaky),

trademarked
all over
with compromise and equality.

I'm the slip

on the red dress
of capitalism—each time
like the first—setting the truth
on fire,   then selling you
water,   'cause, uh, *compassion?*

Still Light, Dust in the Air

Those with a country
must remember

where their
fealty lies—they

cave and start,
bread and wonder.

There is a process
that can rely

too heavily
on humiliation.

It can take forever
to grow out of it—

steer oneself
to light.

All things
happen here

on this try—
this aging

house,
where pride

holds back the revolution,
burning inside.

Fret

Fret

The blue sky, a bridge, we can
rise above this mess. There are things

ain't never left me, like a melody.
We can always

steal a moment, death
trembles

at such
freestyle breakaway light.

Never misses a chance
to remind us

how small we are
and how mighty

it is; the buildings, the beat, the sound
of Gawd,

sussed beneath the trestle
of night.

The birds flown over,
his eyes glazed over,

how can one
not see,

this is how
autocracies

are formed? Some
know better—

their love is stronger. But even they
are not immune

to the draw
of tyranny. If pushed beyond feeling,   if

forced to believe
in nothing. We can always

steal a moment, death
crumbles

at such
freestyle breakaway light. We must be visionaries,

we must
plant trees

beyond our lifetimes. We must
seize the means

from these angels
of corruption, then dance

like dingledodies
down the platform.

Away
from the perfunctory,

into
your leisure—the dusk-ray

night, allegory
morning. I'm going to sit here,

this afternoon,
or take my son

to the playground, become the walls
I can't move, the music

I can't play, the things
I can't say. As he wanders down

the highest slide, checks back, "hi daddy,"
and smiles,

before he runs away. There's noooooo
revelation, only *that postcard*

frozen in time
from history. Meanwhile,

the moment
drags on

in obscurity. The identity
of work itself—

The dirt gravel parking lot
   at my stepson's school,
      reminds me

of the way
   I remember
      my own school

after we left
   Los Angeles—

and here I am,
   tryin' again,
      to coax the night

into brilliance.
   Take the shadows, once more,
      past the paint,

past the humiliation.
   Save my sixteen year old self
      the heartache

that is to come.
   Life is long,
      like a poem

that can't wait!
   Something always
      movin', like those hills.

Take me, mama,
   'round the lake,
      but don't tell me

what we're doin'.
    I want to remember—
        for our son—

what it's like
    to be
        still.

We ain't gonna make it!
but we gonna try,

cling to the beams
of adulthood,

let the kids
ask why. More than broken,

more than sadness,
more than free, I love you.

More like a prairie,
or a moment

so still,
one must

cede
how time

has flown?
From here, I can see

Canada,
then Mexico,

or some new province
we invented,

just past that stand of oaks,
where—because of you, only,

all the cliches
you can't buy me,

I'll allow it:
the ruckus of starlings,

the logic
of sheep,

just one strand of hair, an eyelash, an earring,
and I'm through—

pleading with my ambiguity,
falling like a leaf,

from the tallest oak,
knocked by a rock

rolling towards the ravine.

Up
in the sky,

not a ride /
just a ride,

how could it
be so

monumental
and futile?

It's like
how words

flow, when you're
wrapped

in a tide. If I could just
finish this drink

before this plane
is pulled apart

by space, or my son
knocks

this tray table
down—I made it all

about poetry, and this
is what I

found? Don't
try. Just let the Earth

sound you, like a time lapse,
in this brief

body
of consciousness

and work. If there's one thing
I'd want for you, son, it's to learn

to enjoy
using your hands. You will never be

without purpose. You can always
inhabit

the chaos, yeah,
make it your own, and sometimes rhyme.

If we don't
answer the void

with an affirmation
of feeling,

of life, humanity,
it will respond

with a rebuke
of those things.

Rules
will not work; rules

only add
to the void's

acuity.
Dismissing

the void
or feigning exemption—

that kind of indifference—
is too easily mistaken

for the void
itself, that it hides;

tantamount
to a lie. The void exists

where consciousness meets
immiseration. The void exists

where someone is thumbing
their nose

up
at you. The void exists

on a hospital
bed, in a house

falling
down. And the rules

are there
to keep the powerful

honest, not the honest
powerless. Listen, can you hear

a flower
blooming

against
the void—or is it

just
the rattle

of what
you should

or should not
be doing? Listen, can you hear

the hammer
dropping

in the distance, or did you
just

assume
the revolution

could be
stopped?

About the Author

Jonas Kyle-Sidell lives in Baltimore, Maryland with his wife, stepson, and son. He holds a master's degree in creative writing and publishing arts from The University of Baltimore.

Currently, Jonas is a middle school special education teacher at Green Street Academy, Baltimore.

A Material Rain is his second book. His first, *Reichstag Burning*, was published by Finishing Line Press.

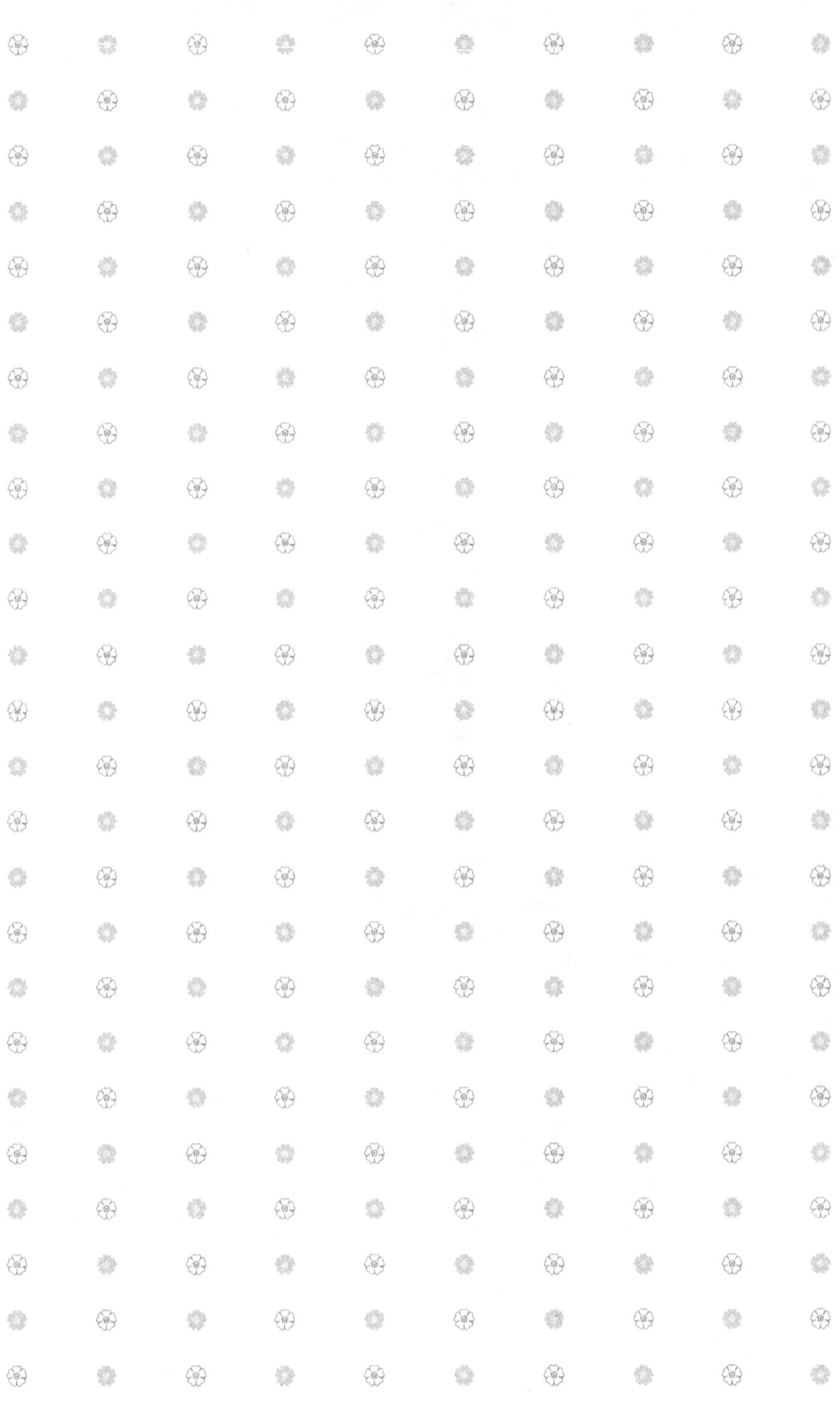

www.ingramcontent.com/pod-product-compliance
Lightning Source LLC
Chambersburg PA
CBHW030415120726
47904CB00007B/2290